IT WAS A SUNNY SATURDAY AND THE FIRST EVER CLAY... DARBY BOINGG WAS EXCITED TO SEE ALL OF THE PLA... AND FLOWERS AND HIS FRIENDS!

GATEWAY GREENING PRESE...

CLAYTOWN FARMERS' MARK...

Darby: HEY, CHRYS! HOW ARE YOU AND THE OTHER MUMS, BUTTON AND POPPY? WHAT ARE YOU SELLING?

Chrys: WE ARE SELLING PLANTS AND FLOWERS FROM OUR STORE! YOU LOOK LIKE YOU COULD USE SOME FRESH FRUITS AND VEGGIES, TOO!

Gateway Greening

Bustin' up Blooms!

CHRYS TOLD DARBY ABOUT ALL OF THE HEALTHY FRUITS AND VEGETABLES AT THE MARKET AND HOW THEY PROVIDE VITAMINS AND MINERALS FOR YOUR BODY.

Dr. Eugenia McFettle: IT'S IMPORTANT TO EAT VEGGIES AND FRUITS TO STAY HEALTHY, DEVELOP, GROW, THINK AND FIGHT DISEASE!

MYPLATE — FRUIT, GRAINS, DAIRY, VEGGIES, PROTEIN

MINERALS: HELP YOUR BODY GROW, DEVELOP AND STAY STRONG!

I LIKE TO PACK VEGGIES AS A QUICK AND TASTY SNACK!

DR. EUGENIA MCFETTLE

DR. MCFETTLE SAYS GOODIES FROM THE GARDEN ARE GREAT FOR YOUR BODY! MORE FRUITS AND VEGGIES FOR ME!

FETTLE: STATE OF HEALTH, FITNESS, WHOLENESS, SPIRIT OR FORM

AFTER BUYING THE FRUITS AND VEGGIES AT THE FARMERS' MARKET, DARBY HAD MORE ENERGY AND WAS BACK TO HIS BOUNCING SELF. BUT THE PLANT HE BOUGHT WASN'T DOING AS WELL.

POUCH 'R US

OH NO! MY PLANT IS LOOKING A LITTLE DROOPY.

I WONDER IF CHRYS MUM CAN HELP.

Bustin' up Blooms!

OPEN

Gateway Green

The Greenhouse

HI, CHRYS! MY PLANT ISN'T DOING WELL. CAN YOU HELP?

HI, DARBY! GOOD TO SEE YOU. LET'S SEE WHAT WE CAN DO!

FLOWER SEEDS

CHRYS TAUGHT DARBY ABOUT HOW TO HELP HIS PLANT AND ALSO ANSWERED ALL OF HIS QUESTIONS ABOUT GARDENING, HEALTH AND NUTRITION.

DARBY WAS AMAZED AT THE HISTORY OF GARDENING AND HOW SO MANY THINGS HAVE CHANGED OVER THE THOUSANDS OF YEARS OF GARDENING AND FARMING.

Nutrition from

FRUITS COME IN MANY SHAPES AND SIZES AND GROW ON TREES, BUSHES, STEMS AND EVEN VINES! THEY ARE GOOD FOR YOU WHEN YOU CRAVE A SWEET SNACK.

Fruits

VEGGIES ARE GOOD AND GOOD FOR YOU. THEY GROW ON STALKS, STEMS AND UNDERGROUND. IT'S IMPORTANT TO EAT A LOT OF VEGGIES TO GROW BIG AND STRONG.

Veggies

WOW! LOOK AT HOW HEALTHY ALL OF THE THINGS FROM THE GARDEN ARE!

the Garden

GRAINS INCLUDE WHEAT, OATMEAL, RICE, AND MANY OTHERS THAT ARE USED TO MAKE THINGS LIKE BREAD, CAKES, CEREAL AND MUCH MORE.

Grains

Dairy

DAIRY LIKE MILK AND CHEESE USUALLY COMES FROM COWS BUT CAN ALSO BE MADE FROM SOYBEANS.

Protein

MANY PEOPLE GET PROTEIN FROM MEAT LIKE CHICKEN, PORK AND BEEF, BUT PROTEIN CAN ALSO BE FOUND IN PLANTS LIKE SOYBEANS, BLACK BEANS AND OTHERS.

ChooseMyPlate.gov

CHRYS TOOK DARBY OUT TO THE GARDEN TO TALK TO BUTTON MUM. HE WAS AN EXPERT ON PLANTS AND VEGETABLES AND THE PARTS THAT YOU EAT TO MAKE YOU HEALTHY AND STRONG!

"PLANTS ARE SO COOL BECAUSE WE EAT DIFFERENT PARTS OF THEM TO GET THE VITAMINS AND MINERALS WE NEED."

Gateway Greening

Parts of Plants We Eat

LEAVES
WE EAT THE LEAVES FROM PLANTS LIKE LETTUCE

FRUIT
WE EAT THE FRUIT FROM PLANTS LIKE STRAWBERRIES

STEMS
WE EAT THE STEMS FROM PLANTS LIKE ASPARAGUS

SEEDS
WE EAT THE SEEDS FROM PLANTS LIKE PEAS

ROOTS
WE EAT THE ROOTS FROM PLANTS LIKE CARROTS

Why Are Plants Healthy?

Dr. McFettle: THERE ARE A LOT OF WAYS FRUITS AND VEGETABLES HELP YOU STAY HEALTHY AND STRONG! FRUITS AND VEGGIES HAVE LOTS OF FIBER AND ARE GOOD FOR ALL DAY ENERGY!

Rocco Broccoli

Rocco Broccoli: MOVE OVER, MILK! YOU AREN'T THE ONLY THING THAT PROVIDES CALCIUM. BROCCOLI IS FULL OF VITAMINS C AND A. THE BROCCOLI FAMILY HELPS PREVENT CANCER, TOO!

Captain Navel: ORANGES ARE FULL OF VITAMIN C, VITAMIN B AND POTASSIUM. YOU'D BETTER BET YOUR BELLY BUTTON THAT THESE NAVEL ORANGES ARE FULL OF FIBER, TOO!

Captain Navel

Carrotina: I AM VITAMIN A+! FOR YOUR SKIN, TEETH, EYES AND HEART, CAROTENE HELPS YOU STAY HEALTHY FROM HEAD TO TOE!

Carrotina

DARBY LEARNED ABOUT HOW THE FRUIT, STEMS, SEEDS AND ROOTS GROW FROM DUSK 'TIL DAWN!

THE PLANT GETS ITS FOOD FROM SUNLIGHT IN A PROCESS KNOWN AS "PHOTOSYNTHESIS."

PLANTS HAVE "CYCLES." LIKE DAY AND NIGHT, THEY GROW, BLOSSOM, THEN DROP SEEDS TO GROW AGAIN!

AND WITH SUNLIGHT...

THE SEED STARTS TO GROW.

WITH WATER...

MY GARDEN

THE PLANT MAKES SEEDS THAT GO IN THE GROUND AND GROW INTO NEW PLANTS!

GARDENS NEED WATER, LIGHT AND T.L.P.C. TO GROW AND THRIVE!

How Does a

T.L.P.C. = TENDER LOVING PLANT CARE

WITH A LITTLE T.L.P.C., TENDER LOVING PLANT CARE, YOUR SEED WILL GROW!

BUGS AND BIRDS HELP THE PLANTS TO "POLLINATE," LETTING THEM REPRODUCE.

MY GARDEN

HEY, I'M BUZZY COMBZ! IT'S GREAT TO POLLINATE!

THE PLANTS GROW FRUITS, VEGGIES, FLOWERS AND MORE!

WOW! THAT'S AMAZING. I HAD NO IDEA THAT PLANTS WENT THROUGH CYCLES LIKE THAT.

Garden Grow?

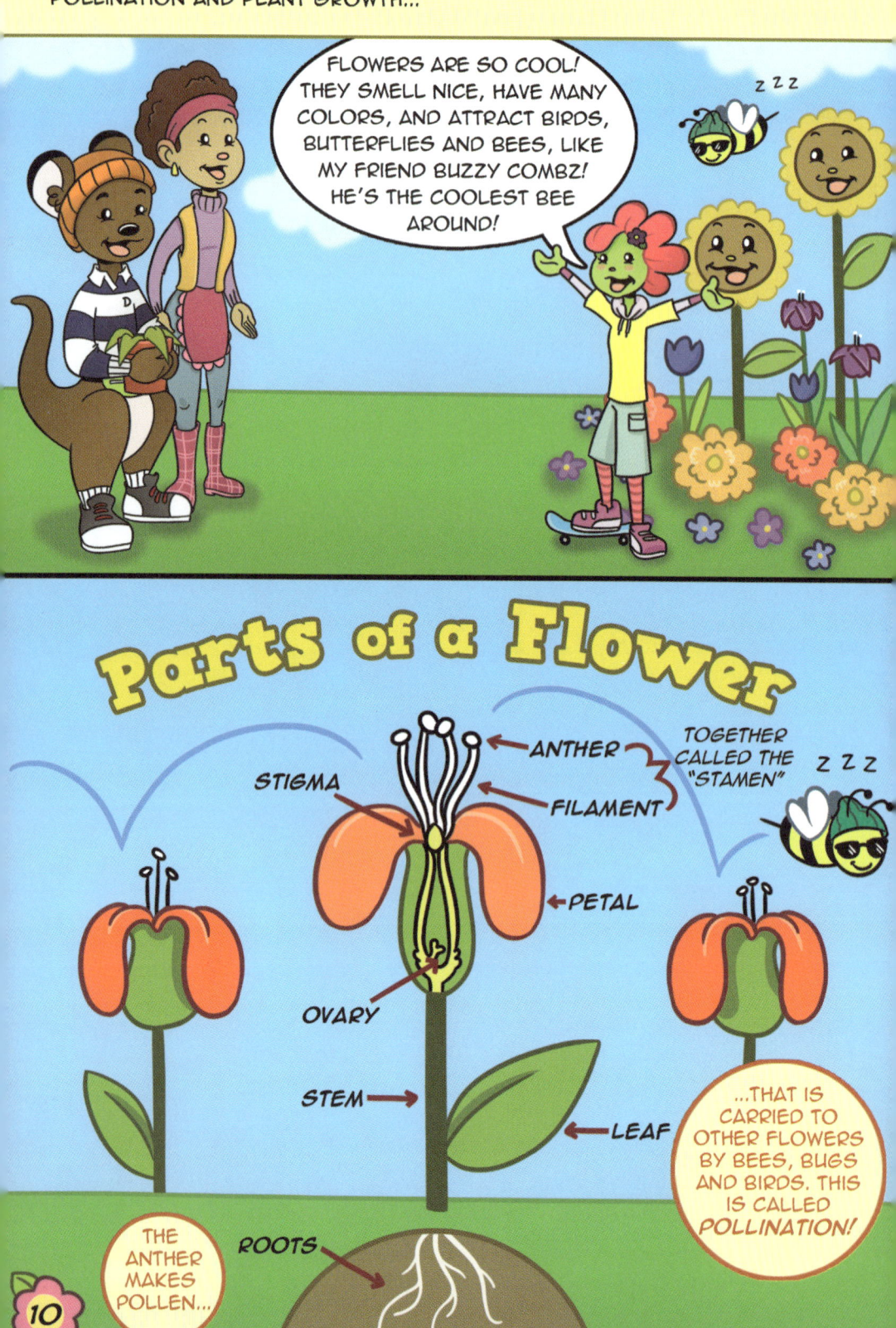

POPPY MUM EXPLAINED TO DARBY ABOUT HOW IMPORTANT FLOWERS ARE IN POLLINATION AND PLANT GROWTH...

"FLOWERS ARE SO COOL! THEY SMELL NICE, HAVE MANY COLORS, AND ATTRACT BIRDS, BUTTERFLIES AND BEES, LIKE MY FRIEND BUZZY COMBZ! HE'S THE COOLEST BEE AROUND!"

Parts of a Flower

- ANTHER
- TOGETHER CALLED THE "STAMEN"
- STIGMA
- FILAMENT
- PETAL
- OVARY
- STEM
- LEAF
- ROOTS

THE ANTHER MAKES POLLEN...

...THAT IS CARRIED TO OTHER FLOWERS BY BEES, BUGS AND BIRDS. THIS IS CALLED *POLLINATION!*

BUZZY COMBZ KNEW ABOUT THE "GARDENING BEEZNESS" AND TOLD DARBY ALL ABOUT THE BUG POSSE THAT KEEPS A GARDEN GROWING.

YOU'D BE "BUGGING" IF YOU DIDN'T THINK BUGS WERE IMPORTANT IN GARDENS.

DID YOU KNOW THAT IN A TEASPOON OF DIRT, THERE CAN BE MORE THAN ONE MILLION TINY LIVING THINGS?

MY OFFICIAL NAME IS *DANAUS PLEXIPPUS*, BUT MY ROYAL SUBJECTS CALL ME QUEEN DANA. WE MONARCH BUTTERFLIES POLLINATE MANY PLANTS WHEN WE MIGRATE OVER HUNDREDS OF MILES. WE ALSO EAT A PLANT CALLED MILKWEED WHEN WE ARE YOUNG!

I'M STILTZ THE SPIDER. I CAN BE DANGEROUS WHEN I BITE, BUT I HELP IN GARDENS BECAUSE I EAT BUGS THAT HARM PLANTS.

I AM GENTLEMANTIS! I EAT GARDEN PESTS, BUT I CAN ALSO CATCH AND EAT MOSQUITOES THAT ARE PESTS FOR PEOPLE!

I'M MISS LADY, BUT I'M NOT ACTUALLY A BUG! I'M A BEETLE, AND I HELP GARDEN PLANTS BY EATING PESTS THAT ARE HARMFUL.

VISIT **MONARCHWATCH.COM** TO FIND OUT MORE ABOUT MONARCH BUTTERFLIES!

I'M WIGGLE! WORMS DO A LOT TO HELP GARDENS, BY DIGGING HOLES THAT HELP AIR AND WATER REACH ROOTS!

I'M STUMP! WORMS ALSO TURN THINGS LIKE LEAVES INTO NUTRIENTS FOR PLANTS, AND WE DO IT JUST BY EATING!

Where Does Your Garden Grow?

Water Garden

WATER GARDENS GROW IN POOLS OR PONDS.

HUGELKULTUR IS WHEN PLANTS ARE GROWN ON PILES OF ROTTING WOOD.

Hugelkultur

MANY DIFFERENT TYPES OF PLANTS CAN BE GROWN IN GARDENS.

GARDENS ALSO COME IN MANY SHAPES AND SIZES!

CONTAINER GARDENS ARE WHEN PLANTS ARE GROWN IN POTS, BINS, BARRELS AND MORE.

COMMUNITY GARDENS ARE GROWN BY GROUPS OF PEOPLE LIKE FRIENDS, FAMILY AND NEIGHBORS.

Container Garden

Native Garden

NATIVE GARDENS ARE GROWN IN THE WAY PLANTS WOULD BE FOUND IN NATURE.

Community Garden

Gardening by the Numbers

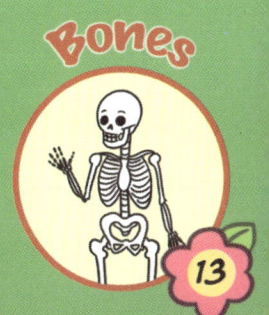

PUSHING A WHEELBARROW USES 27 CALORIES EVERY TEN MINUTES!

WEEDING USES 150 – 157 CALORIES PER HOUR!

PLANTING A GARDEN USES 135 – 177 CALORIES PER HOUR!

DIGGING WITH A SHOVEL USES 150 – 197 CALORIES PER HOUR!

Flexibility · Joints · Heart · Bones

DARBY'S HEAD WAS BUZZING WITH ALL OF THE GOOD THINGS ABOUT GARDENS, PLANTS, VITAMINS AND HOW HEALTHY GARDENING MAKES YOU- INSIDE AND OUT!

"WOW! I FEEL LIKE I KNOW SO MUCH ABOUT GARDENING NOW! I THINK I WANT TO GET MY FRIENDS TO MAKE A COMMUNITY GARDEN, WHERE I WILL PLANT MY BASIL."

GATEWAY GREENING Community Garden! Plant Time!

SO DARBY AND HIS FRIENDS DECIDED TO PLANT A COMMUNITY GARDEN AND GET IT "GROWING"!

USE A **TROWEL** TO DIG IN SMALL PLACES LIKE TO PLANT SEEDS.

USE **MULCH** TO HELP PLANTS GROW AND TO KEEP SOIL MOIST.

USE **SHEARS** TO TRIM PLANTS AND CLIP WEEDS.

WEAR **GARDEN GLOVES** TO KEEP YOUR HANDS SAFE.

USE A **SHOVEL** TO DIG OUT PLANTS OR MAKE LARGER HOLES.

Composting

- SCRAPS
- COLLECT
- PROCESS
- SOIL
- GROWING PLANT
- FOOD

TRASH IS TRASH, RIGHT? WRONG! CERTAIN TYPES OF TRASH, LIKE FOOD SCRAPS, CAN BE TURNED INTO SOIL THROUGH A PROCESS CALLED "COMPOSTING." ONCE YOU EAT FOOD, COLLECT THE SCRAPS AND PUT THEM INTO A PILE OR A SPECIAL BIN. ALL OF THE "INGREDIENTS" IN THE BIN WILL HEAT UP AND BREAK DOWN INTO SOIL FULL OF NUTRIENTS TO HELP NEW PLANTS GROW INTO FOOD THAT CAN BE COMPOSTED AGAIN!

From Farm to Table

FIRST, PLANTS ARE GROWN ON FARMS IN LARGE FIELDS.

WHEN THEY'RE READY, THE PLANTS ARE HARVESTED.

"FORK" in the Road Farms

SECOND, THE HARVESTED PLANTS ARE STORED UNTIL THEY'RE READY TO GO TO MARKET!

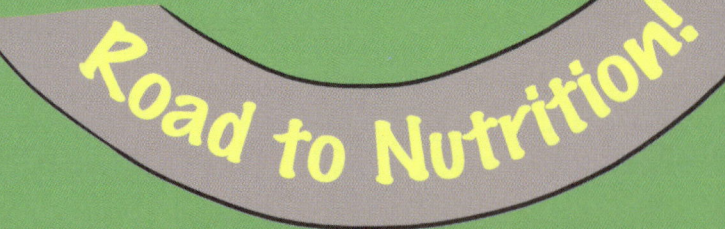

Road to Nutrition!

FROM THE FARM TO HIS PLATE, DARBY'S CARROT HAD BEEN GIVEN TENDER LOVING PLANT CARE EVERY STEP ALONG THE WAY! DARBY KNEW THAT T.L.P.C. WOULD HELP HIS PLANT GROW UP TO BE IN THEIR COMMUNITY GARDEN.

DARBY THOUGHT ABOUT GROWING THE COMMUNITY GARDEN WHILE HE WAS EATING HIS VEGGIES FROM THE FARMERS' MARKET. AS HE CHOMPED ON HIS TASTY CARROT, HE WAS AMAZED AT ALL OF THE HARD WORK IT TOOK TO GET IT FROM THE FARM INTO HIS BELLY...

Get Your Garden On!

CLAYTOWN SUPER MARKET

THIRD, FRUITS AND VEGGIES ARE TAKEN TO THE STORE.

BASIL IS AN HERB. IT'S USED A LOT IN COOKING MANY TYPES OF PASTA. DARBY NAMED HIS WALLABASIL!

LASTLY, THE FRUITS AND VEGGIES ARE BOUGHT AND COOKED OR EATEN RAW!

DON'T FORGET TO USE:

T. L. P. C.!

TENDER L♥VING PLANT CARE

17

Get Going on Your

AFTERWARDS, YOU CAN TRANSPLANT YOUR PLANT IN A COMMUNITY GARDEN!

Drain water
MAKE SURE THERE IS A CONTAINER UNDER YOUR GARDEN POT TO CATCH ANY EXTRA WATER THAT DRAINS FROM YOUR PLANT.

Water
YOUR GROWING PLANT WILL NEED ENOUGH WATER, BUT NOT TOO MUCH.

CONTAINER GARDENS CAN COME IN ANY SHAPE AND SIZE!

Garden Growing!

Pat Dirt
WHEN YOU PLANT YOUR SEED, PAT THE DIRT DOWN OVER IT.

HOW WOULD YOU PAINT OR DECORATE YOUR POT?

Clean
AFTER HANDLING YOUR PLANT, MAKE SURE TO WASH YOUR HANDS OR USE AN ANTIBACTERIAL HAND CLEANER.

BASIL

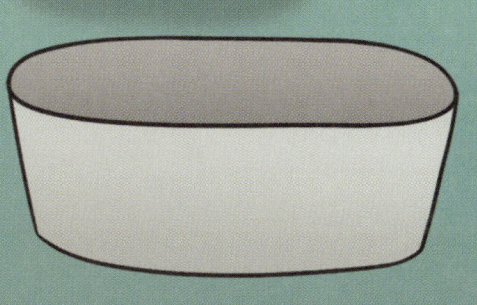

SOAP

My Garden Journal

DRAW A PICTURE OF YOUR PLANT EACH DAY AND WRITE WHAT YOU NOTICE CHANGING. DID YOU NAME YOUR PLANT? WRITE THAT, TOO!

Day 1

WRITE YOUR PLANT'S NAME HERE!

WHAT'S "GROWING ON" WITH YOUR PLANT?

_____

Day 3

WHAT'S "GROWING ON" WITH YOUR PLANT?

_____

Day 9

WHAT'S "GROWING ON" WITH YOUR PLANT?

_____

Day 11

WHAT'S "GROWING ON" WITH YOUR PLANT?

_____

WHAT DID YOU NAME YOUR PLANT?

Day 5

WHAT'S "GROWING ON" WITH YOUR PLANT?

Day 7

WHAT'S "GROWING ON" WITH YOUR PLANT?

Day 13

WHAT'S "GROWING ON" WITH YOUR PLANT?

Day 15

WHAT'S "GROWING ON" WITH YOUR PLANT?

Word Find

FIND THE WORDS IN THE LIST AND CIRCLE THEM.

```
W H D I O B L D E G U S
P L A N T S G G I L G O
B L D U G O W L A D F I
U G L D U G A G L D U L
G I L A I E T E A L D L
S I D L G J E O D U G H
S L G U D H R L D U H X
X C S U N L I G H T L W
```

Words
SOIL
PLANTS
WATER
SUNLIGHT
BUGS

Spot the Differences

FIND SEVEN DIFFERENCES AND CIRCLE THEM.

Connect the Dots

CONNECT THE DOTS THEN COLOR BUTTON MUM.

Color the Container Garden

PLANTS COME IN MANY SHAPES, SIZES AND COLORS. COLOR THE PLANTS BELOW AND DECORATE THEM WITH STRIPES, DOTS OR JUST DIFFERENT COLORS!

BLOOMER

GREENZ

PETALS

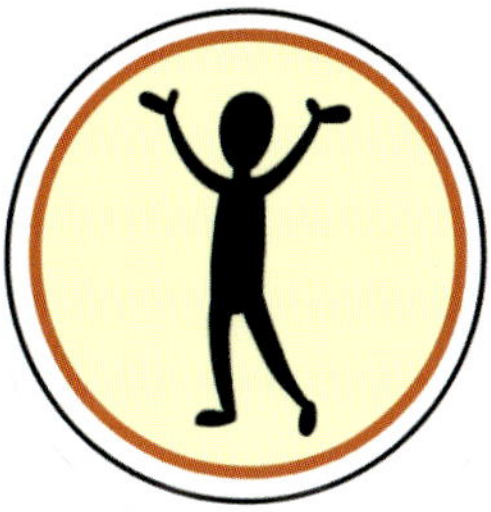
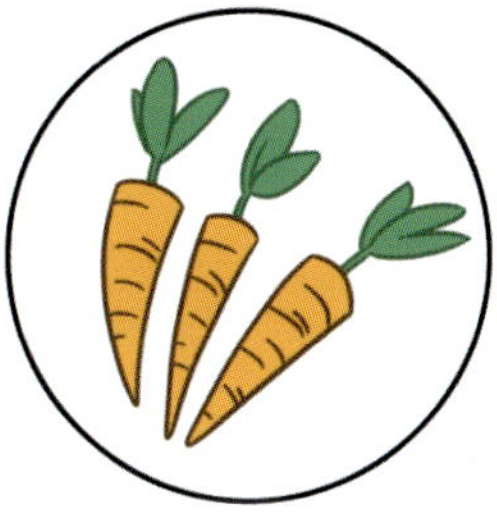
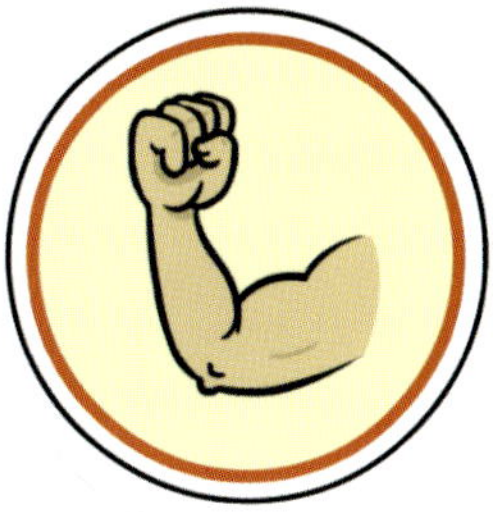
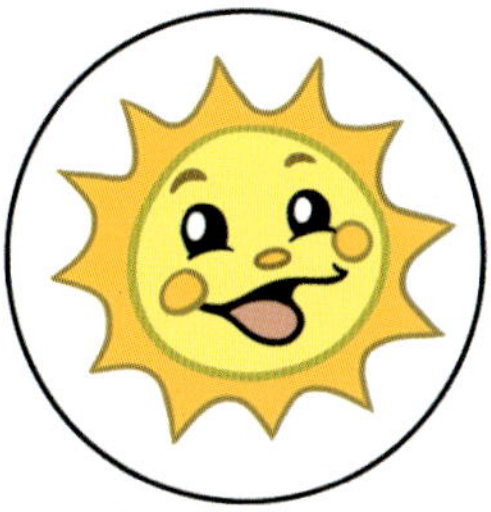
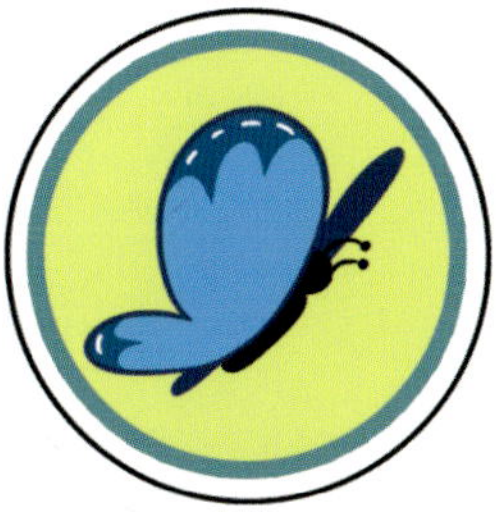
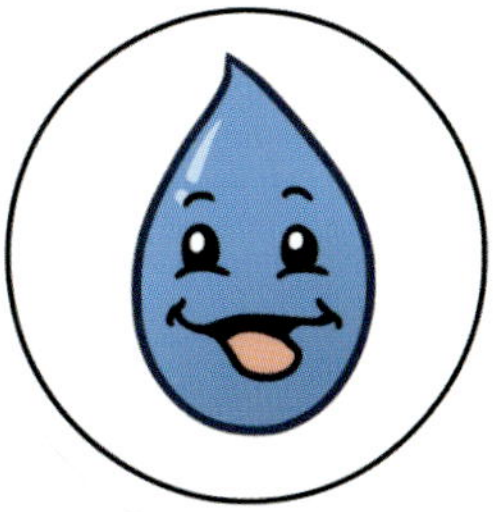
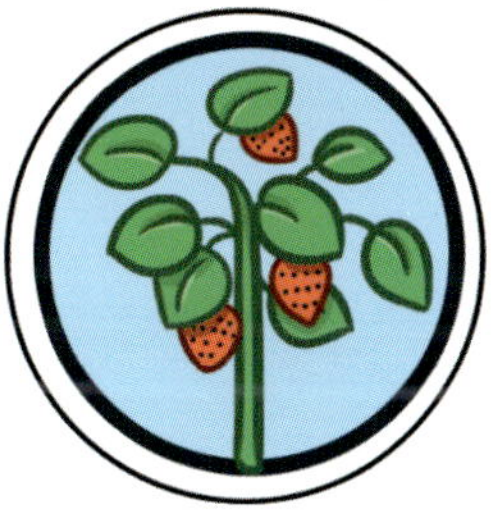
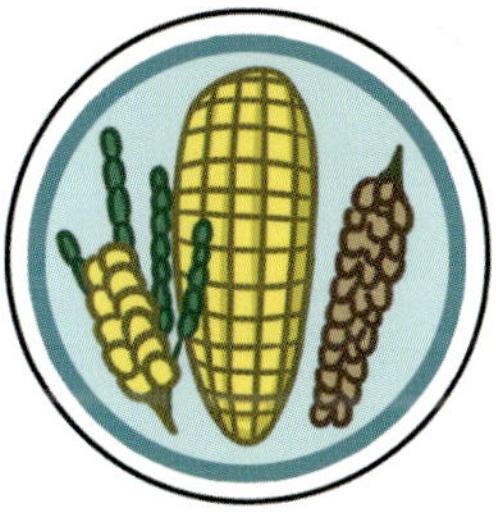
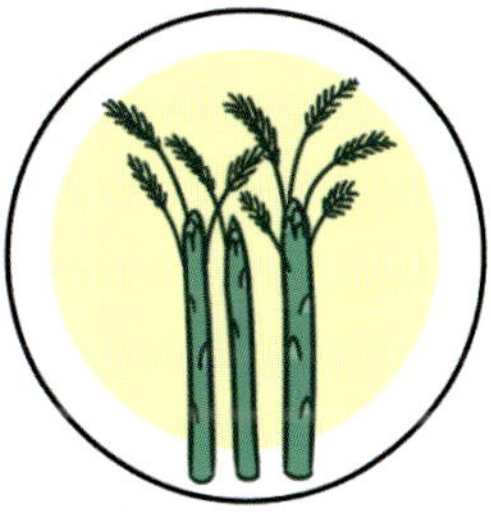
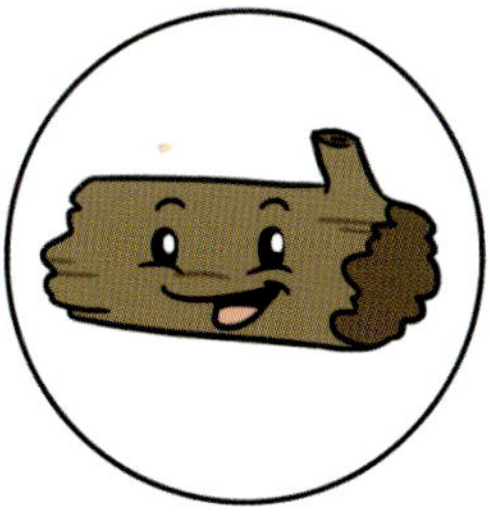
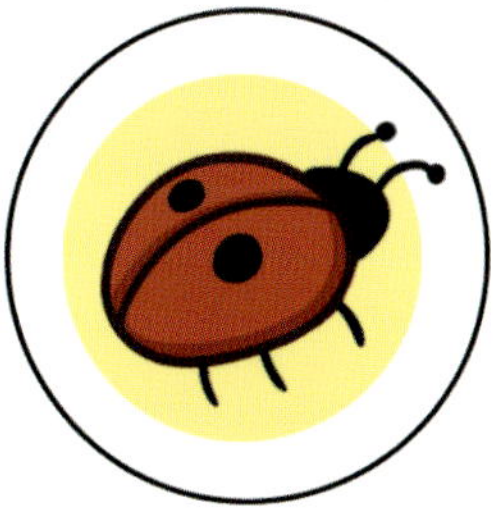

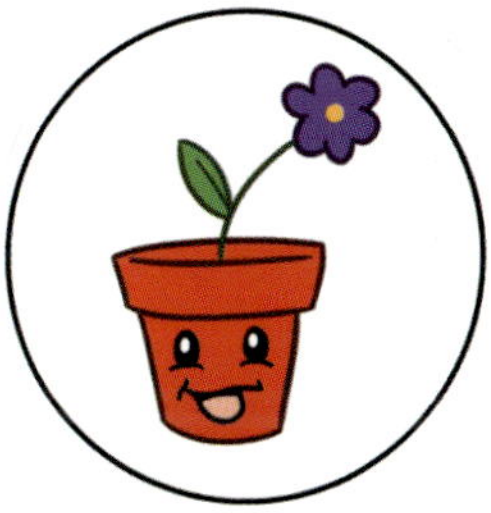
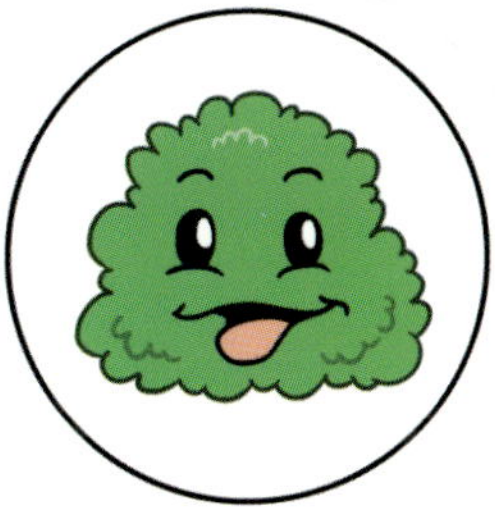